The Ottawa City Project:

poems by rob mclennan

The Ottawa City Project:

poems by rob mclennan

Ottawa 2007

Cover design by Tanya Sprowl
Layout by Jef Harris
Cover art by Kate Seguin-McLennan

printed and bound in Canada
by Custom Printers, Renfew, Ontario

Chaudiere Books
858 Somerset Street West
Main Floor
Ottawa, Ontario
K1R 6R7

www.chaudierebooks.com
email: info@chaudierebooks.com

Library and Archives Canada Cataloguing in Publication

McLennan, Rob, 1970-
The Ottawa city project : poems / by Rob McLennan.

ISBN 978-0-9781601-6-6

I. Title.

PS8575.L4586O88 2007 C811'.54 C2007-902270-7.

for

Wm. Hawkins, Michael Dennis, John & Susan Newlove
& my mother, Joanne Irene Page McLennan

Contents

you are sleeping
in ottawa
it's another hot night
after the fashion
of steam and tendrils

– Judith Fitzgerald, *lacerating heartwood*

no more capital capitals
– Stephen Cain, *Torontology*

My pa was an Ottawa guy; his whole family was and is, really. Though I have been here longer than anywhere I know those streets of yours from riding my James Reaney bicycle along every one from dawn to dusk in search of something.

– Colin Browne, *email dated 26 October 2003*

ottawa poems (blue notes)

Outside the window, the world lies.
– Erin Mouré

1.

from backwood lumbertown,
    an exercise
        that works out of progress

where main street so far off the main

brandished, a tradition
of contemporary

back a bit

    the pool cue over

bank street from the lip
of parliament hill
          all the way

roll south to st lawrence,
under another

no one body
        or poem
    remains the same

mayor, governor
general, prime minister

& other optic
failures

2.

i people this room, this
small apartment
                                        on somerset
w/ telephone calls, letters, books

a damaged photocopier

a small voice inside the constellation
of friends & journals, ideas
& bad memories
                                mostly good

a voice
            inside a whisper

, a human value

to combine
into a consequence

3.

samuel de champlain,
                                        nepeans point,
                          a bad taste in the mouth

a couple performs rituals
             of first fumblings of sex

a deed of gifts: personalities are charted
by naming
                          : bytown, lebreton, mechanicsville

past & present
, heartsore

old ottawa south,
             where pushed

the city down

                                        the prescott hotel,
in 1934, what once
last chance, deliverance

fore city line (they say); that way
lies madness

, suburbs

4.

in spite of knowing
                            & not knowing

a january walk / the winter sun,
the soul of fire

didactic breath, speaks mouth
as function – ottawa,
              an insult meaning politic

what we call ourselves, w/out
much choice
                            regret
                                               a city
              of degrees

dark water over rock
construction
                    the champlain bridge

a documentary feel; mark marsters
a finger
                    a map

on transit rock face

5.

after all these years,
where do we go

dutifully planted bulbs, & waited
patiently for spring

a scar or backdrop

a wheel spins under ice

6.

short letter
        & the long farewell

new bedrock of belief
                to fill in silence

a road is not a road, it is
                the bushes & trees, the buildings
        & the parking lot, it is
                        a fiction

norman levine in sandy hill,
gazebo where he rested
                in the shadow

        of his mothers apartment

slow enough to enjoy the telling

a city i have been so long w/in,
w/in me too,
                dead hospital
where mum & i,
thirty years apart
                        the grace
        of endings & begins

7.

a poem as the city,
we talk
a single line

continuous of the long, completed
only now
& never

two days a whim of taste
along the sparks street mall

forever opening & closing

the tunnel rumour
from hill to old american embassy,
or chateau laurier,

overlaid upon the real

ten seconds of wonder

8.

the nations capital,
long seen as front
of government drones

a falseness

& cosmology of bureaucrats, pulsation
& desire lack,

palpable

the days themselves accumulate,
through colonization,

a process of estrangement
& the continuous story

the beautiful long

briefly on the bank,
& glassy stare of hull,
the gatineau hills

my own hand
goes trembling into

9.

as much journeying in making strange,
beyond this,
                                        the centre of government

parliamentarian
& visiting dignitaries

                                                                        the city
shut down
when president bush

or the car
                                        barrelled up
the parliament steps,
                                                        ignoring
lampmans lines over wooden doors

this is there, & there, charting a series
of stories
                to inform ones own

paul chartier when
                                        , late 60s
                who planned to bomb parliament,

sitting quietly the next room,
& blew himself up in the bathroom

instead

; i regret the omission

10.

a tangle of events

not spoken

true & not true,

dependant always

upon who is speaking

beyond the capacity of history
; a speaking

unencumbered by the pressure
of lyric closure

caught

in blue line light

wild bill hawkins
& his *ottawa poems*, nineteen

sixty-six

to whatever degree

& the demands of biographic

11.

if any city,
by practice & definition,
a prose tradition of houses
& 19th century rock
given the hunt
& justification,

to never let go of ecstasy

i remember the end of meaning,
& the extension of the queensway

projected foot bridge linking somerset east
w/ somerset west

, centretown
to sandy hill

another straight line of groceries
& long maps,
turning his head
to be informed

half concrete, grey & unutterably cold

what a river runs erratic
through

12.

as have been claimed,
            the ottawa river
                        named for the odawa
a more recent band
on traditional algonquin

                                    , as had moved on

things get lost in the desert

three days to cope w/ sky,
during halleys comet

                        does anyone remember; best
& less foolish

to simply admit the snow

13.

call each visit a lyric,
                    or lone construction,
        where there is so

; of brick, no local
stone unturned

                    what quarry emptied
for either version of buildings
on parliament hill
                                        , a perfect mould
                            carved down in earth,

        in canadian shield

what more we move, a treatise
on the political creatures we are,

        according to tradition   :   in winter,
                                                when dark so long

                              at night, so cold, held tight

her seminal body

14.

anyone who opens their front door
                                        w/out reluctance
          possibly recalls

, the brains wired music

recognized the singularities & such,
ambient up lebreton

          when once the jazz fest, folk

w/ fists of lawnchairs;

                      the public & political hoopla
mean almost nothing to the ground below,
the feet

          who walk there; discourse

definite in the universe

a city goes; a city

          ; no final stanza; people

15.

every june or so
the fire hydrants
get repaired

a line of brushes
south on bank
, a bucket of white

& bucket of yellow; like children,
carting crayons

the centre & the impetus
& world & the creator

do you, in this case language

ramones t-shirt or furnaceface
todd gibbon of the fiftymen

a light on the floor of the commons

you pack your bags & call it, *thus*–

16.

i wasnt quite ready,
a poem that a bird could light upon
w/out suspicion

a poem in a city

the falcons nest on top
of world exchange

blue marble following
the path of sun, or is it
the other way around
draw lines
as you would other

a train to montreal
, or drive out to pontiac

a mulligan, a mistake
in golf

the reader, unlike historian,
must construct around these gaps

17.

a stretch
to cut across time
: the ottawa river

the rideau

canal, a
deliberate swath

i sink my sights on
you dont have
to understand

each line of blue
an *accumulation*

of concentration, colonel by

particularized by these injuries
on rock

a blue light on the shore
, salvation

a ferry under alexandra bridge
a faint hope of redemption

18.

i am thinking of that dark line
that hangs on the edge,

queen elizabeth drive
an echo
by trudeaus eyes

1974, before
the growth of trees

change & a continuous,
the university
he blinks
long after

a cadence suggested geographically
from popular burlesque

to question period,
the end
of the line,

the rhyme

19.

the water boiled

someone throws a frisbee
in major hills park
in 1992
milton acorn sells books
in front
in 1970
the list is endless; listless

& planning figures react to mud
& exhausted budget
at the birth of buildings

landscape parliamentary sludge

brief fountain before flame
eternal only

from the start

one steady finger to the moonlight
one steady finger

on one side of your face

20.

if ones esthetics
& ones ethics
are conjoined
in a task both serious
& of use,
what does a city

what does a town once
series of neighbourhoods
& still,
in rockliffe park

or where the poets are,
beechwood cemetery,
archibald lampman,
john newlove, & even
tommy douglas

beauty seen in justice
& a right economy,
poetry
& people

& lyrical swoon

what did i tell you

somehow, they survive
these people, these women & men

on lampposts, grey
& gentle

21.

a roughneck past
of self-definition,
editing in

, speaks of a condition

a baseball fan, a multiple
a hockey fan for some
a football once, a nearly
forlorn goal

something that w/out,
their doing damage
to one another

the late frank finnegan

in the middle of the day
i found myself
at the ottawa exhibition,
landsdown park

& move now w/ a song
of buses opening & filling
& azure sky near fit to burst

a blue-white blur of air

22.

the body of both,
comfortable in our
regular world

the city of ottawa speaks, the poem
is listening

& failures come, pressing
on our sensibilities

as much as anything

a trick w/ a knife, & snow
packed under ice, what i
believe, or feel

a forlorn goal

in multilingual soup

the reconstructed plant bath
, a breath of perception

concern
of belly & lungs

perhaps for this reason

23.

this is not toronto
nor anywhere else,
the hole
that must be filled

& no longer self conscious but still
breathing, conscious
of our fragile beauty
& cold uncomfort

lady lady i cannot lie,
not just
or only

the little brother, too close
to shine

a likewise arrangement of trees
black-winged birds
a cloud of pigeons round
apartment floors

at cooper & bronson, sweep
glorious around

waves of down
wind,
grey

servings of rain

24.

the end of the line
                                              or is
            naked in our recreation

caught in a music of sparrow-warmth
& dislocation
                        a walk on the canal

simon a drink a drink a life
at the carleton tavern

            without you on my mind

so the poem is not a description
so the city is not
                                              a grey slate
            floundering

                        the beauty of
                                              the unseen, or
            unrecognized

the bread-line should not return

                        as the city goes,
one encounters wit

i have remembered this little
poems intent

            unknowing too in mixed metaphors

25.

comfortable in our shoes,
the thin blue line
of cabs
like cops & buses,
the semi-precious,
never around
when you need

every day is always done,
he lies in a heap

in white stars or space

because of the storm, because
it is a living fossil, still

the city of ottawa, lives a path
, what did i tell you

& repeat

in looking at the palm

where we love our buildings such
we empty
, renovate
& abandon

the lampman house b&b

when are you thinking of disappearing

26.

save the bad news last
& the good
intoxicating songs

might provide a start

everything i dream
in black & white
in colour

the hand sewn naked

wire of your march
through the glebe

my once apartment there
or old brick house
on rochester
, the heron basement

as much as is accumulated
, lost
& perhaps more

the line of homestead
bramble hood

of sticks & stones & maps
& brochures

27.

an acoustic of geography, cultural
argument
in winterlude
or bands
in confederation park

the tragically hip
outside the city hall
previous to this

jane siberry new edinburgh

out of long lines,
pinecrest
greenbank
a cemetery

on both sides;

it is important to observe

, poetry
& formal history

speaks, but they are
not the same

28.

          all cities
                                        like poems
                    can be biased

for omission / transference of sky
& peace tower
                                        , what hour
rings twice

          a shadow
                                   we will feel upon
what then a city is
or isnt
                    walks by a bus
but never enters
                                        , tourists
          camera the byward market
& wellington

                                                  , i
                    stay close to home

29.

shaped like a church steeple
stand up straight

smile like you mean it

    if this is a house you entered

billings house & billings museum
& all the land around it

south of the bridge

    the swans, a gift
    from queen victoria

        & their descendants, populate
        the waters edge

a haughty grace, could break your arm
as easy
            if you get too close

30.

the storyline
has prompted,
a documentary impulse

a take on the falls: chaudiere,
a basin
at the rapids

moves quickly, & so much
moves slow

the view from here, brought
up from earth

a roadmap of the vital

31.

the light on back porch
laughs
            a cobweb
of later trees
                        a hill
looks down the path

of rail, & rail remains
i stand down at the rail

historical accounts of leaf
& sediment

the arts court building, ceilings
filled w/ horse hair,
                                    peter honeywell
            the days he pulled at it

original outline, door
from 1850s

to register marriage, birth & death

; what they would step through

covered;

                        window
                        , brick

32.

sentiments of the fire
& fire
                    the more than one

erased a city back
; last daytime of the eye

to founders then, i announce
my lack
            of indifference

half past laurier
                    , a quarter
    past booth

        would let me know

to purchase out a loss
, the hills & air

or kingsmere, mere
a truth & err

        to structure is design;
        to care is ruin

so he asked himself
; his mother, dog

33.

a personal region
　　　　　　, interface for fear

economic only

border subtle, point
the centre in

by first account

paddle leaves
& then the lake

from montreal
down

a portage path
　　　　　　, held open

mining light
　　　　　　, too much

a silence fan

34.

if you could walk expanded
in a borderless

transparent

, omeara
down elgin walks
& thinks
a simply called

what going on in country
is
what going on in street
or city wide

a crashing tide

jealous of demands

the building on somerset, beside
the beer store
, where
the cold war sparked

the hooded spy, gouzenko

, a plaque

or gladstone where they played
the stanley cup

no rink in sight

; a laundromat, a plaque

eroding years away like teeth

35.

if progress
remains an illusion,
banks close
& their buildings

heritage empty, or
sell wine
a busker
at frozen doors

a city is as flat as a page
a city is a four letter word

i am caught up in will

that the archives file away & drown
once i am down

the streets
of a living city, living

living for its own sake
the whore of babylon
of barrymores

of zaphod beeblebrox

why do these women
break my

make that
, what

36.

across these margins
light moves
centretown a dark
turned wheel

benjamin chee chee traded drawings
for another drink, the
gilmours edge

the bottom of the pond with mud
was not so much the same as this

, intending

hang the day out to dry

meanwhile i watch the people
bank & gloucester turn

a parking lot a bullet pushed
brian smith hard, deep
in harder ground

a crossbow on argyle,
if
you cant hold on

so much happens now that doesnt

37.

there i was standing

corner nates deli or further down
a scene involving caring
            & the soul, a weeping of indication
& silent knowing

                                    , saying nothing

a head full of snow
& sewer marks

an episode   ;   i cheat
                                                   in blank space

the parody of living, what will
                    one day be yours is suddenly

                    yours no longer; fled

still standing

whose city am

38.

if i dont need
to satisfy
, the mouth
of ottawa to outaouais

two rivers, kissing

open stone ; if it
figments an homage

if i had meant to cross a boundary

everyone has their favorite act,
everyone has

their favorite prime minister

arthur meighan

astronomy was cold

the cold on the hill & the liquid
& stone

& champlain, pointing

out like a fool

39.

she said around 1920
or was it 24

        architecture of organic

the church they married is still there
but not the house they lived in

at 607 maclaren, percy street
divided into slides

        apartments where they knew rooms

wind carving trees, & paths
for mayors

        long as a ledger

house hold (city) earth

I want to toughen
my attitudes
on mediocrity

& make a few statements
on values
to the crowded busloads.
– William Hawkins, *Ottawa Poems*

bank street

a line drawn south as far as river goes, from parliament; a maple leaf on spine
s j jarvis photographer a dog on corner smiling smiles; letter
an entry; crushing writing to restraint

a long a city street, a main line line, dissecting bank facade, dissecting groceries
through south & south & glebe & keys & suburbs & the city fades away &
anything goes

something you might miss; think a general economy

a signature of snow & rain & mornings; santa claus parade or gay pride; you can
hear before you see
there is always something to do; walk down
to post office, post office, royal oak pub which one
is real if even any are; irenes further down or alta vista where it meets & grandma lived
her forty years
on ridgemont

back north closes wall street, what we were somehow trying to do, like; the conditions
themselves cry out wind tunnel dust, dusty north just of somerset, the bruises
up business & windows, an open door
covers

if you were articulate you would know the road; think a general autonomy; a greek wheel
a paste-in; bridge a river gasp; a dwell
promenade, you know ive up & down been sidewalk, sales
ive never seen

dusty light on probing hatred; a shallow
street main,
main
a map line

leans up to stone

number two bus

through communities, an east end shopping centre & a west
through chinatown, little italy, westboro, the byward market, low income
housing, vanier, heritage buildings, the collusions
through bank street promenade
through highway commuter traffic & the far flung edge expanding city
through every red light
through every moment
through every remarkable delay of intent & circumstance & wanting
through the little place that sits behind the eyes & watches
through the poems disappearing fading slow from banners; ronnie r brown or john flood, mine
through all the hyphenated city sections; a place a place a placelessness; how
does a city make; where hyphen holds a memory, a link
                                                                                    to further shores, little
          glengarry my apartment; little glengarry archive & a little secret
through the flat line of the page
through delays & delay; twelve minute schedule, up to twenty minutes late
through cloud
through routine & ripening
through singing; the flesh cant wait

a shore is not a demon is not a thought of transportation, public transit we are
all public, displays of affection & transportation; look at where im going
i just dont know; dont ask me to choose
a pragmatic sequence; articulate
                                                  a talk
                                                  a speak, speaking; buses are they big enough to double
articulating speed; spend tickets or handful of last change or change; whatever it is it is you are
my mother remembers centretown streetcars; &
                              in some places you can still see tracks but nowhere; erased
          an erasure
as you would sing a little hymn; the red & transpo white a maple leaf
an eric walker reproduction black on black on bits of metal, wood
solution to so much other, other, in
across the road or two

bells belt a line a whistle stop i pull, collect;

almost weather, groundhog day

amid the favourable winds, the day the same movie every year, bill murray
this year the rodents contradict; wonder
            whether memo got
the chandelier
                        , complain abt the cold in peterborough, hardly a day goes by
the ottawa snow diminishes; sun down, long in the saddle, thinking

if music comes from listening; if music comes from the imagination of the building
eyes tight shut on planes & angles; l'esplanade laurier is white it is still white
it is off-white, still

envelopes i have to purchase, a package out i have to package
out where words resist, the snowplow on the sidewalk takes out a tree

maybe the method heaved w/ delight but i dont
maybe the slopes were slow to go

if spring comes now is winter far behind

fairmont chateau laurier

old link in cp chain when the hotels back
had basements in their stations; ottawa, calgary,
edmonton rail
laurier house, & dear
wife zoe, you can get a drink a cup of tea in the
piano lounge, afternoon fingers
getting close
last of the cbc holdouts, the past among
as old as radio itself, moved out then into a thus building
of their very own,
alan neal
sounds so much taller than he is but friendly

new copper roof slate oxidizes brown to
eventual green, rain lines paint already down the outside
a lichen stain

like so many others of its time; designer in the day, old man
titanic down in 1912
another old story telling story, so little new being told & discovered

his body a wash, a wash of plaques & portraits in the lower halls,
what you know & you will
know again
what whispers
in the elevators & walls

it is in this way that stories are told & retold

by-ward market

a pigs head or a shirt of beads; angel & a devil locked
in a car my best girl
                                        , the dominion tavern
below the strip-club; night we after hours
                                                    i am listening
to a number on a locker; listening to a punk band live & living; light the
ceiling goes
               a market by & by; to ward off any anger
ward off any fear, so far
         successful in its trade, a focus
bars & clubs & shops, the mall, the rideau
                                  walkway, bus mall, busy street

isnt a city allowed to change its mind

               think of the thunder ahead
ottawa bagels when they were close to best
& all night, late remains
of any day, the place where language reflects
in the shape of a coin

english & french; french & english; a binary that ignores
the expansiveness of so much more

                         across the road or two
in lower town, a market of one where have
been more, the current parkdale, former elgin
market building, where once city hall (1849-1877)

a city
where archaeology so much level ground, stand
to satisfy, know, the hustle
                         of any market city; crowded streets

the centre of all human interaction & activity

winter, winterlude

what layton told, in winter where the nights are long, we
          warm each other in our beds
the nine months after the eastern blackout or the ice storm
population booms

                    when the lights go out,
we build, & grope, the second
coldest capital,
                              celebrating winter
instead of hiding in our homes
as i
                    sculptures of ice that every year
either solid cold too cold to see
or begin to melt

          of festivals & forty below, a city of bureaucrats
& government levels nearly endless beneath the storm

                    , fireworks blow
above where men roll dice & wonder; reach out for a hand
thats never there; the break of day
                                        , a crack
in river ice
                    ; every year like clockwork

a snowmobile & a boy go under; somewhere up the valley
          breaks a heart

summerlong

I am not a man & this is not my city.
– George Stanley*, At Andy's*

summerlong & weve barely entered spring
where is spring, what happened, you say in your emails

the mind is more frustrating, my head & my heart no longer speaking
        the same language; tess when she was here, tess of montreal, the beaver
& the totem pole she saw by the canal where she was walking
what locals never see or look
                        the thought of this
& sweetness, all the dreams weve had & history, grown up tween chinatown
        & sandy hill; the layers go strata down to bone
& other centuries
& the hours rooms that even now you separate

summerlong i am screenplay love
& lore

this is not a bad city nor a bad country
i keep myself out of as much trouble as i can, although
not always possible

the thing of yr lips in the rain along somerset
the sting of rain w/out capitulation to the grain as it washes,
wash away & gone

spare moments: seventeen (failed) ottawa ghazals

for phil hall & michael holmes

You have lines linking starts to stars
As if the illusion
Of nothing between them is an error.
— *Fanny Howe, Tramp*

BETWEEN THE BODY & LANGUAGE
a ravine of call & response

if you look down the well for the moon
your head eclipses the shine

hurting myself is a still they'll never find
— *Phil Hall, An Oak Hunch*

quick ghazal while waiting for kate in the tim hortons, rideau centre, february 11, 2006

the sum of the very coffee,
invective cold

the scrape of days take winterlude
from muddy water

to bare bone

how every curse at the bus stop
a silver shadow

a forced migration turns dyspeptic

my mutton heart arrows
a hangover of trees

her william tell overtures

the days of cholera & new york magazine
covers

home a figure for mixed meanings

we wound by how

we name

quick ghazal while having breakfast at pubwells restaurant, preston street, february 12, 2006

the forlorn sweeps of powdered snow
across womens hockey

the noonday sun bears bright
, italian down

catered boundaries; an elongated shore
of sidewalk; familiarity will erase

yesterdays *globe & mail*
a couplet lies

womens speedskating, elvis
costello, hockey

from the plant bath (table
of twelve); a brokered salvage

of highlights

there is little space on a sunday
for the spontaneous gesture

or the spartan fact

quick ghazal while waiting for beef shawarma in the shawarmas king, bank street, february 13, 2006

asymmetrical, a drip
of morning shine

& shame

through lucks blue romance,
the frost can coalesce

insubstantial, or substantial then

the static of bedrooms
& an itchy trigger

thunder bronze, the sweet air
struggles moisture

a candied sticky heart

if a defense against death
is an exhumation

hardly a defense at all

when they come march swallows
back to roost

the voice is neither throat
nor song; stalled

half-ton sediment

a photograph of self-respect

quick ghazal while waiting for the tree reading series in the royal oak II, laurier avenue east, february 14, 2006

reflected in plasma screen

a lack of silver
in that silver sun

dark wood & circumstance; dark wood
& sheath of snow, waves

as we drank & we drank

a heart attack of collaboration, shavings
as the trials place, bets

to unsnap like a seer

the sirens on reflected windows
burn red

living tuesday memory
& a bloody valentine

a fast-moving cigarette at the end
of no river

a champion of all things
concerning no-one

quick ghazal while waiting for friends at the carleton tavern, parkdale market, february 15, 2006

a spare sign, tinted windows

from red neon glare, & low slated speech
; days the shape

of a deliberate pour

artichoke lungs & liver, three ribs
on the ladders rung

broke, bottom

from here to the floor, or
furthest wall, what

a lungful of fresh, torn awake
amid famous americans

happy, & some

would want simple perfection

the brokered broken cash machine

inside; the cue to the kitchen,
pool

& juke-box

a single celled question grows
, picking at soft skin

quick ghazal while waiting for the montreal bus in the greyhound terminal, catherine street, february 16, 2006

beneath the battered wind, a selection
of dry ice

to find a living stone

bent down to the face, a babys
breath;   blue shafts of snow

at fifty frames a second

each name on the timetable map
a fragment

of a fracture; secretive,
& still

& lie like a second reader

beware the ghosts that line the margins,
fingernail the underside

, threat of generations
& the intertext

across the midday sun, devices plunder

heart to a snow cloud; cosmopolitan
& the local

time is entry, & misgiving

a groping ground zero

awash in gulf stream february lungs,
held cold or a cough

quick ghazal while waiting for a drink at patty bolands, clarence street, february 17, 2006

the guinness glottal pause
, escape

a word works wonders

to a hamlet of discovery, at the southern tip
of the first floor bar

thick crate of celtic, barrage
of oak barrels, lidless eyes

carnivorous voiced balcony
, the look-down, lock

our blood & theirs: a thirst

an empire washed ashore intemperate,
a roll of one by one by one

a single tab, stephen

makes up for it

two edges w/ her silent driver
& bare shoulders

way down below; an inkling wretch

a third & final last call stretch

quick ghazal while waiting for the movie at the world exchange centre, albert street february 18, 2006

a lackadaisical air; escalators turn
, fill the basement w/ steps

hanging nardwar, folding beauty
in suspended air

a three day glisten

from shape to signal, youth is captured
on a ticket stub

between child & adult, in the difference
of a single cost

an escalating scene; if hudson
filled w/ holes

a preliminary flicker, or fate
worse than fact

engine trouble

; a whispering word as winter weighs
discoloured breath

sun scrapes the length
of pre-recorded beach

securing playback

, the tides

quick ghazal while playing phone tag with lea graham from the front of my apartment, somerset street west, february 19, 2006

laughs lost in driving

a cambridge deadmans float
of cosmopolitan, just big enough

to turn around twice

a mudhill clasp associating borderlines
of typeset brown wrap

the pin-up; in a beautiful car parked
only; small circles

an ash upon snowy sidewalk listens
w/ capital g

as many times as you recall

& driving, says: avoid beginners; dont overlove
what you love; what you

know of your dagger hand

a staggered letter hails a one-arm second; sweeps
corners in compressed time; a red car

eradicates

conferring left signal bright in the back

widow moon arbutus at length; muted soundscape
of central mass

    if she found what she was
    looking for

while two clicks, four weeks hence

quick ghazal while waiting for bhat boy at the starbucks, bank & third avenue, february 20, 2006

when here be dragons, dragons
or waiting

a commercial culling front; shipping island

a starbucks across / from itself

    of the oldest neighbourhoods,
    who are

a flood of any little surreality,
red parliament dragons

    such olympic particulars
    can hardly be blamed

& red brick century   ; post-war
in terms of how to live

    if the bobsled and luge
    share the same length of track

of never-known; mechanism
of battered colour

    there is snow welded melting
    the soles of my shoes

a glebe fable, park
where the art lives

quick ghazal while waiting for fresh coffee at the second cup, bank & somerset, february 21, 2006

a tie times margin,
still at the hearth

delay, delay, the time
indomitable, will

threat of needle, damage done
& the spoon

the boys are leaving half
again empty

a carcass of afternoons,
a car crash distills

hard wire, secrets

from controlled burn; a lamp out
buckles under

extreme stress will not make
for crater lakes

or dusty promenade

after two full days, my body vibrates
still

the directions that making end

quick ghazal while sitting at the computer in the back of my apartment, somerset street west, february 22, 2006

a weather of creaking steam, frozen canal
from a spring board

thrown regional dice

boundary water & blasted journals, late capital
plunge; a montage urge

in the belly of commerce

the trees where the dream is; a syllabic
of potraiture

not in technique but in doctored flag
on rural mailboxes

a character of dented aluminum; the kind
of coffee once breathed

I am half-then; there

in terms of a scar we would
never mention

an angry mab of horses

an inquest of boundaries
; the river ; degrees

in perilous transit

shoveled home
in a dismembered anything

from four wheels on carbon spin
gone ground

is it winter we want; is it spring

quick ghazal while listening to gryner + stochansky etc perform at the national archives, wellington street, february 23, 2006

irregular intervals, a footnote
struck by thought

or remakes, big in japan

open, like a guitar case; piano
, glenn gould on the smaller stage

to overturn serenity; & call it
another

as valuable an emotion
can be blessed by soundwave

round robin lift; the present tense
is rapturous, rapt

& skin

in due submission

her dulcimer tang
floating westward, north

I remember it because it was me
, from this blue light

to endnote; a glorious tide would tempt

quick ghazal while waiting for monty reid at the manx pub, elgin at frank streets, february 24, 2006

the artifice; speaks to city hall
& precision of 1812, the war

nose nickle number; no snow, handle
to justify the side

in poems on straight lines

a concrete example of canyons press
burgundy curtains & plant

the bootstrap

when next about how
the world, & procedures

coalesce; forgive
in tender entries

corners of the craft so precise
or coolness,

said he, who dug coolness

a line of flowers; falsify touch; the olive
branch of grace

a gravity of preserves

an empty panhandled wretch in oil
, significance oversized the frame

a dog talk
walks, & suffers under

sees drink; a terrible
yank of sternums fourth gallon

slow ghazal while sick at home
in my little apartment, somerset street west,
february 25, 2006

, mating chainsaw must be deaf

, w/out mercy or a toothbrush

, a clerical error must be sought

quick ghazal while waiting to speak to the unitarian universalist fellowship, loyola drive, february 26, 2006

of folding chairs & excess, folding chairs
& gymnasium banners

tropic & a full veneer

a scar once sewn so young
, as accurate as hell

if you believe therefore & choose

torn by the backdoor, remained
a hard crave inversion ship

other sorrows if reversed
, a candles dying

of unseen interiors; tantalizing
score of heartspin

goes out the foregone sad, crumpled mercy

w/out syllabic warning or static

a buckshot senior bridge

quick ghazal while waiting for the boys at bethell field house, frank street, february 27, 2006

as paul says, the weekend
where he lives

a significant streak
of white light windows

& last considered fall

shattered, a recovered sense
; of white-hot rooms

token through, violet; drizzling
outside snow, turned sideways

on its monday ear; a film
morning recovers

blue in the sock-drawer face
; diary entries shorthand

to the limpid shore

I am every day reveling more
in the adolescent past

like a latchkey dial,
descending

descendant of needles & crumbs,
an underground claim

a track of maritime laughter

cowled, & caught on

each moment further, a sap
snap loss of natural light

a day progresses

shipbuilding (or, the white journals)

, a suite

words words words the words

law

again

winter

and snow closes over
ottawa grey city
the city

a book closing
a closed white book

– Eli Mandel, *Stony Plain*

these examples hold no water
but a life is worth documenting
piece by piece

for example: *I'm not worried*

– Julia Williams, *The Sink House*

Sir William Logan, from the Report of Progress for the Year 1845-46

Supplying ourselves with provisions, we were enabled to forward them up the Ottawa first by steam propellers to Bytown, and thence by steamboats plying on the Lakes Chaudiere and Chats, with the assistance of wagon conveyance established at the portages as far as the Falls of the Calumet, a distance of about 175 miles. Four Indians were hired at Caughnawaga and, with the aid of the gentlemen in charge of the Hudson's Bay posts, at Lachine and the Lake of Two Mountains, we obtained a couple of excellent birchbark canoes.

river poem

from montreal
from the lake of two mountains
from lachine
from the river grande, the ottawa the outaouais
from champlain to the hudsons bay company
from hawkesbury
from buckingham
from the northwest traders
from ottawa, hull & the chaudiere
from eb eddy, booth
from chats falls
from ile caunet & fort coulonge
from the rideau canal & petawawa river
from elizabeth the queen victoria
from horse trains to the steamboat trade
from colonel by & hands that made
from madawaska & bonnechere
from mattawa & the mattawa river
from lake nipissing & the french river
from her exposed shoulders down her spine
from the end straight back to the beginning

shipbuilding (foundation

you were writing a paper on marriage
& wherein lies the question

, a question of lies

i was working on a poem
on the ottawa river

how you cant step into
the same truth twice

arriving too early for dinner, i read
an essay on homemade beer

by paul quarrington

you couldnt work with me in the room
i tried not to laugh out loud

at the essay, not at you,
half a glass of merlot

i could tell that you
were not impressed

i pictured a lemon, the shape
of an hour

field, between wake & grace

(a western quebec poem

a solopsistic range, border is

entreating, acting out
or strange
                                        ; *i mythic,*

a juried system; trees,
rocks, squalor, stone

fits & starts; a pontiac brush

a line of land a language a border
water trips

the black sheep, three times
in

templing, a knight
in shade

the men are; men here
menhir
                        , drinking export
drinking fifty; how

many men

to bridge a long-gap; encircle
binary gestures
                                                , aboriginal

not algonquin but before

village cape particular, strafe
a down striation

river rapids river river

is but one name,
holding

quick ghazal on the manx pub

she steps a pint across
unbroken line.

the hockey game again,
game six.

named for the island, cat
a clipped tail.

david in his blue blue shirt
becomes the sky.

her kathleen edwards t-shirt
is nearly new.

quick ghazal on bank & gloucester streets

the immediate world exists
at right angles

the intersection where the bank,
office towers, tim hortons

in the throes of service — public
& private — plastic picture tags

on strings

the rain puddles out
to biblical proportions

what cabs tear by
plaster multiple suits

the day we lost the stanley cup

would that we knew nothing
of sixty silent years

against a long, perfect season

of lower-case capitals, a flick
of the wrong wrist

puck white against black

so close could taste, of iron
in the blood, a blue line

of the heart

so what of next year

a spring of perpetual blame
that could lose us all to hockey

shipbuilding

if i am to discover anything abt you,
it is in the space between words

i will apply all knowledge
to this simple step of learning

the mail-steamers that rolled
from thurso to ottawa banks

the ghost of madisons war

i am littered w/ pieces
of scattered fact

you ask for the names & the routes
of my former lovers

            , these differences

become semantic
                        , i would rather

lean into a kiss, would rather

the water from the river flow
around us, hard

& unabated

reduction

a hole in the side
of 3 storey brick

labyrinthine rooms, a rugged
cross-section

blocked off, by day
diminishes

& night

abandoned slow, before
it fell apart

opened wide, a mouth, seems
larger than it was

the house on gilmour, once
overrun w/ squatters

& sudden cops

to take away what had been
torn

the duke of somerset

an elegy

edward seymour, the duke of somerset,
for a secret marriage

over edward vi

the corner of bank,
where the banks were

the duke of somerset pub,
sixty-eight years

in the same family

not a tavern licence new in this city
for decades

now one less more
where less

is exactly that

where will our old men go,
to smoke treason

of cigarettes

or warden
the scottish marches

one more disappointment

headless
at tower hill

pubwells, preston street

im from lake placid, he tells me

the songs of lucinda williams, i dont
need to be light

last week, they threw handfuls of snow
at matts window after midnight,

& it wasnt matts window

the mornings correct themselves; what then
the light shaves

swat team, house on fire, ambulance; turn off
the front step

half a block, jerry drives

dark glow across the moon, sinking
down these few lines

if you lived here, you would live
in an empty pub

ive been here since 1958; he says
he thinks he says

when someone asks you what you think
its because

they want to tell you something

whether you want them to or not

a new bottle of jaeger, & then mike
the new bathroom

sleep the canyon of little italy

if only we had nothing left

shipbuilding (summer lovin')

when the british fleet went stronger,
fewer asked the white pine

a wheel & a spit they would lower

what am I, the ottawa water down
& sappers bridge, pretending

a two-ton breaking stone

slow pitch on brittannia, the log
boats roam, long before a means to an end

& precisely an end to itself

if river then, or white; a populated stretch

the pure spring at caledonia,
where princes, kings

a century gone

at minto, underneath the ice
where skaters then

would find them spring; or muse
where she lifted

the summer is draining away

the address book (erasure)

for my mother & her mother, too

This is not a description
Of my feelings about
The trope
The torrent
The forged address

Crushing vial
Blew me back
A long way back

I should have been listening
To every word you sang
Rapt pious chant
— Nancy Shaw and Catriona Strang, *Cold Trip*

233 gilmour street

my mother own & baseball diamond, home
aint what it used to, last rites of houses
then not so, set & set upon
runcible, mountain high & the street
contained everyone, tender disgust
& cicadas sweet rapture, august moon
of red summer silk contradictions, plastic light
of fathers, her own a cold cigarette
plantation, stroke or no stroke, a
form of erasure; snarl of smoke
suspicious materials, brokeback colonies
anticipation of shores upon shores upon shore
once speaking clear, they moved; obtain
a clearer speaking picture, gilmour torn
& torn down; immediately moved
their material restriction impeded, & built
in nineteen sixty-six a tall brown
oval ship in harbour minutes, impressive
& leaving them no lesson to meet

30 spadina avenue

bandied about a heart, a heart of pearl glass
minute of slippers, a balcony rescue
, rotting couch, a nylon viper, catgut
when she sleeps, our frailest sailings break
& slow dead microphones; the weight of slender wire,
burrows daylight flung in space, a fourteen-inch
, a fire-hiss, sneakers orbit
full of mud; where we born soundless, electric snap
& wall of all our possibilities

30 pretoria avenue

the last place I would thought of, home in art
represents the deepest cut, the catabolic plane
in thinking of an atmosphere of gratitude; remember,
when we comfort; swans in the river once, & taste
of wind in breaded hands; a symphony of noises small
& as themselves, introduce the world; the entire universe
is as much there four walls, small hands reaching
popping cheerios & quilted cloth, till burst & beaten, where
there is no buckshot gravel or composure; the last show picture
small town snow a shovel on the front steps, plastic cups
of needles red my life in art; it presses cookie-cut
against itself & pulls; I am bloodied a likely dream

96 rochester street

a portrait of our findings; phone lines break the manes
of horses wild; like a hardy boy blue leans cautious
& a smugglers cove; homemade wild basement bucket wine
& longshore fears that beat the current hooks & tides
beyond the angular cells, beyond the clumsy signs,
the drunken birthdays, parties at the bare bone of listening
; a history of narration; when we sleep, we sleep inside,
quietly disbanding; a kitchen counter note of passage,
quick cautious halo sips; rain obeys gravity & grace;
my fingers lose practice, communal lip of cauterized trees
the backyard planted; dark watered deck at night
of your foreboding; or if like antlers,
the berkshire horse was all we left, a paper trail, a stone
encased in ice; each year a year, a starved gaunt
twisted & eaten, drifted over; who wrote our own way
into immortality

6-25 de la roseraie

a final year of destinations, when purged themselves
of content, incompatibles; a legend in the sky,
back bare a heated window scars a mercury rush,
a certainty of grilled light; if between the blues
unknowing trees, replace hair w/ snow leaves
a logarithmic residue; the kind of singing
cats make, contemporary & delicate stirring

1067 heron road

youthful shoulderblades, a pilgrim
meets an obvious rock; the big wind approaches under,
or fact-finding farm, cry ararat! all the sea
in his swaddle, or swagger, beyond something precious
or reviews; a lock in the door is a lock,
but a key defines only; I would whisper this,
I would two heads kick coloured balloons from the billboard,
carving beatle legs down, & be spilled
three-legged carpet; would she, from that tear in the moor,
won a garland or window, oh circumstance
, what a difference survival man makes
in a marriage; in a day after day after day
w/out nightmares, astride the good power
& a kiss that looks only ahead them w/ wonder

1293 ridgemont avenue

three times they moved & three erased,
my grandmother & expanding diminishing brood
from hawthorne to gilmour fifty years to kirk drive
do you remember; crawled full length to back
another poplar down & trees in treehouse
weak too weak for getaway; a bellied push
of thin encroaching ice; two named; house
that we house knew, expanded for the rooms
she could dead husband neverlong be
clouds moving, disbanding; extra rooms
& kitchen too, a big wind footnotes timber
the beauty of closure & a basement
full of toys; the playboy calendar every male
cousin knew; in her arms, in her grand
motherly arms as deep as my own sensibility
she heat in still air, pencil caught
& like a mountain, runcible high & lethal
caught in the end & when the time caught
moved, again; flowers in every room, reduced

2622 equus way

held aloud, a letter from the first floor beaten
, planes above; a lake full of steps
& soft skin; the news in black print black stars
& scars, the news from moving light
that never made it; panic pure of visitor strays
& in whose shining begins; he fears the cell,
the cellular, amount of tourist mouth creates,
an evidence of burrowed down in cabinets,
filled w/ yesterdays writing & the letters
from long encapsulated dead

607 maclaren street

when first born climbing a pole a hundred neon years
a birthing agent to the east, a moose creek; married a block
of twin spires; does she blossoms fall, or crack,
of unclean boots or meanings in the way,
dark embassies there of poloroid conclusion, a drink
in his altars, a whole brow furrows, weaves
a small post in a living storm, mementoes,
& outlives, outlives; she who stands still tall above them,
green grass sentinel, chronicling outstretched legs
& is least afraid to die

1156 wellington street

would you never think, to ask about appearance
from a darkened hole in empty ground; the phone rings
through reading moon & sun, a quarter displaced yard
& breathless chants my very first; as original day
creation sat, morning sunday born, shedding skin on skin
we had our work cut, full; lumbering intentions
two by two, a trick played w/ the light, &
histories of mice; not only aspirations but autonomy,
a unique twist of style; an obsession of need,
philosophy of streetcars & her siblings names, I suppose
the same taboo applies reverse, the mountains north
& south & valley fled; am sanskrit, an obvious age,
& if the building gone, pushed ground, a dip
in parkdale field then filled, was any ever really born at all

1284 kirk drive

blooming a primary objective, house
is still a house; fields farmer chicken fed
approaching outward; last day of the move,
the street & sidewalk clear had names & name,
concurrent; what sat amid gilmour then & next
but fixed foundation; the end of city, seven children
& the slide; a twist of mason jars; a shining sunset
boulevard; the farmers lips moved corners
of his mouth; coloured prime, the dandelions
true hue, cut across lanes & simple lines; did I tell you what
develop meant; at once he finally
farmered on, the street changed numbers,
married names, to ridgemont, as suburb houses sprung
& blossomed in his fencepost wake

128 st. joseph blvd

if ground in action; gun store johnny,
lights sprinkle christmas insertions, describe
imaginative ice-floes; the flower & the asphalt, asphodel
an hours compliant, walk footsteps small & battered
in a fruit bowl, bottomless; I have been there
& she raised her voice, painted hands
& her arms & legs, her breathless
properly comprehensive; lions & tigers & zebras,
spontaneous rituals of eye & the local, lace
of rust & ruin, engine of unique beauty, breakable rub
as sand presents to skin; would cut my hair
& women they become; each day, a thing
routine of light; a bleed of bestiary, shaping goblets
made of blameless tongues; the lips move noisily,
slip sometimes; her coming years & through the flames
her whisper-storms, her sleep held rafters, arm
& hammer by the bed she kept, a tokens-reach

189 hawthorne avenue

the first point what I've heard; out like the bleed
of broken tiers; clumsy signs & enforced idleness
seashore sticks, a happiness did not miss
an even tension, begins; would bristle
& embroider, enough a break-up, swim to mainland
water brims; the shadow of seasons & the matchstick
, men of hours, off; houses & castles, wooden blocks
accrue; if she is pregnant, would; my mothers sister, snow
from rafters, fence & trees, where there are these
no longer; & when they left this time for left for leaving
so too was struck; lees avenue ramp & soldier
student ghetto, drink & vitriol, whole wheat
mountains arranged of middle english, bare
what is bare, & still is always lyric snow, self-conscious

---

unnamable plenty, the cross cut spent across the further wall,
a corner bent in morning prayer; a thistle first,
a bee, held back for tension, hiding almost
in roots of berries meant; bombshell, blonde & jaundice
yellow of a bruise spent amplified, guitar-picked
veins embroidered time; a mouth caught open
playing stages that were even smaller, could a street east-west
be long enough to hold, foot bridge in the stars,
projected; your anemic breakable bent
& hard-pedaled heart; as delicate clean as hollywood, music
sings out sacrificial, ordinary love; been I have
denied full measure; beneath a tree would suffocate
the universe root, a mountain score reflects
the flatness; dearest flower, invisible; I want to be
that kind of man; promethean fire, outside the higher court
dust settles

586 mcleod street

it was scary sudden; doubled up w/ rain, become
its famous face; balcony thin of round ends thrown
sweet water through; I had a talent once
for uneasiness, when red said no
& the red said; nothing could have walked out
fire-storm & fled, unmarked; to dream
a sandy waste to innocence, water drunk on wheels,
orbital-thin, prefer one points & nine months
sweet, a seagull season bliss, one winter
viper-stone would slowness turn, a mirror only
scant w/ holes & lumbering; so sudden,
as I said, & broke like pieces home
& shattered; assume a void & brighter visions, smelt
w/ six hearts; burning holes, the table lamp or
broken bowl, the work gets complicated; borne,
burdened, done

1500 heron road

into her final days, a bendable, tall & thin
out just one moment, drafts; a blister, we are
amateurs, in song; the silent movie score
piano fingers offstage years, & years
she played us, occupied the noise of palms
& bulrush; words themselves seek nothing, apartment
bound, important foreign works & rotary phone
a pleasant parting; ice & earthquakes, mountain
high & airplane lifts; we are condensed, & live
accordingly; bore her decades out, children
& their own; a broken house
in fragments still a home; in autumn, street noise
shakes from body, mind; her english bones
& red rose figurines, collect she never made of spoons
& schoolgirl cures, her parents wedding china; eagle came
& every morning stole her memories, mind, an irish
stone beneath her shanty-tongue; as each day back, then
fewer grew

the (ottawa) lectures

Bergk says the history of a text is like a long caress.
– Anne Carson

address to the ottawa chamber music society, 2004

what i long for is impossible, the curve
of her calves

like any american soil

three glasses of wine,
as i watch her long caress,

fearful for her high heels, falling.

what happens in this room, stays
in this room. undone.

you say you were, you say
you are, ten thousand strings hum

the national gallery, water foyer.
blue sculpture paint

& finger on the shutter. look here,
& then look. it will

soon make its presence perfectly known.

lesson of the modern nomads

made off with an airline safety card,
glossy, overside stretchy-road
a centred rhythm. intimate human details

i watched in the news. but the news
doesnt give, beyond
the full-colour pages, beyond

glossy overtones, beyond
the self-explanatory title. i admit,
i never understood. i admit,

the sentence languid as a rhythm stretched
long across the country.

lecture to the religious tract society, 1866

for gwendolyn guth

end product of naming, a woman
with a tin ear; tin woman

wrought, w/ perfect pitch

above saintly death, scenes
of pious children

& strong women

a history, contemporary
of emily dickinson

& some, checked in
right away,

a night

to heed such a call, a
heroine or such

if not sufficiently oiled,
the revolution built both on faith

& industry

lesson of the combination lock

what would this be called,
third address or the seventh

if it ever leaves the note

this is a lesson in low-fi, a construct
of lost volcanos & waterfalls,

painted on the insides of matchbook covers

this is an experience in minimalism
& linearity

of aesthetic possibilities
& commercial breaks

, it is

address to the carleton literary society, carleton university, 1993

i have always preferred hallways to auditoriums,
pubs to theatres & podium,

a gentle gravity of aqueduct,

& national embrace, we stand on guard.
this is a library w/out books, listen

to these empty pages, who speak as well
as anyone. the dark skin

of wild beasts. how

could we not shine, or fall, or tumble
out into the square root of green,

trees sticking up out of us not careful.

lesson of the chaudiere

what artelle cant convince,
every poet here

from confederation on, composing lyrics
on the falls

a century & a third
of grey

george brown a statue on the hill
gone blind

mike pearson in the wakefield soil
forgets

water rushing, rushing
over

will still be here beyond
these petty lines, these

petty favours

contained but some
by eddys wake,

a mess of stone
& foam

lecture to the bathroom mirror, november 19, 2004

knowing the difference, we fall helpless
into air

any indication of the blue

fifteen years a city living,
a neighbourhood a home, shifting

soil under blocks

lebreton bedrock

construction crews foundation shakes

when could be lucky in there; leaving
bad boy hair & game of golf

always was a religious art form

of any petulant couple

lesson of her apartment, spadina avenue

for wanda

what once mechanicsville,
& boundary rail

rochesterville

no man is an island, or
a woman

a peninsula

an isthmus

what lack of wisdom is,
or in its own way

the empty park, for children
too young to know

sweep of her car, &
sweep of skin

her empty attic, &
her empty bed

address to the patrons of dorans hotel, wellington street, april 1855

with the arrival of the steam line,
a new era begins

for our long squalid town
, impressive on the banks

of the native river

if a fight begins, as long
as it doesnt spill over

to the rich homes, sandy hill,
the cops wont care

& nobody gets hurt

the dark sky, candles
& stars

& politics, a
devils play

if a temperance society
out of tomorrows ash,

so be it; until then,
raise a glass to the rail

, the night soil
brushed right from our shoes

lesson of the ottawa waterworks, 1876

the year we entered the 19th century,
a bit behind

the normal school & waterworks,
the year of house to house delivery

from postman

a foot of water waits

the creek or sewer finally covered
, line through byward

the worst of winter storms, 40 centimetres
of snow

a bottle of brandy,
nip of medicine

or so

, the city fathers

if could impart ourselves,
we would

lecture to the ottawa press club, 1899

despite what they tell you, lampmans purse
isnt all

dusty shallows of sparks street,
streetcars bell

& whistle

church windows will explain,
in stained glass, a scarlet letter

among lines

but much more innocent

another glass of brandy, another
glass of scotch

if you will

punctuated

what horses kick

lesson of the unrequited

never count on anything, the egg
before its hatched, you said. could

you be any more.

too much complaining for no reason
would not endear. a paper fracture drawn.

hand
that you handed me

withdrawn.

address to the city of ottawa, 1857

so this is newness; so this is
bytown, gone

victoria queen her hand upon

listen to what the land tells,
ghost of a shattershot; listen
to the earth

while it is still earth, muddy
on your boots

a canal is something but it is not all

macdonald still knows nothing
of minimalism

or the light touch

grain alcohol & cork-town
; every exit is

your horses & your
last resort

lesson of the cattle castle, aberdeen pavillion, landsdown park

we will [not] be abandoned

lecture to the national capital commission, 1967

where these natural boundaries evolve,
through water

where you cant get lost

north, where the river is; south

a green wall of trees, a ring
enclosing central

canal & green, or mooneys bay,
to keep the airport

when the sky fell

engines rise
& descend, in turn

a deliberate arc

from the peace tower
to old ottawa south

the hunt club road

perpetually begun

lesson of the fire, lebreton flats, april 27, 1900

nothing lasts; everything
connects

bridges gap & fire house
made out of wood

water is no barrier

address to the carleton county by-election, 1832

what did you think, gentility
was a made-up sum,

a military out

old hammet k pinhey, who would
lend his name

to pinheys point

an obscure outpost
of ottawa sage

& sundry clippings, pressed
to leave black eyes, the wind

from mens guts, out

of lower canada,
opposite

the jackals lynx

late spot, that under heaven,
each man thought theirs

& theirs alone

the cleanest

lesson of the rideau canal

after alan cumyn

built for the invasion force
that never arrived

the lessons of 1812

& all of that, skating
as far as you could

the battle
at chryslers farm

or lundys lane

at forty below, wind chill
in faces

& long up their backs

a population of thousands
inch of pale

scott, of the antarctic
or bytown

by this alone

a city of optimists
& romantics, away

from the bureaucratic edge

lecture to the ottawa improvement commission, 1911

as our sir laurier suggests, a new vision
predominantly as capital

& centre
for intellectual development

let the sawmills die; between
a great industrialist

& stately

water power for manufacturing,
& a horse

or electric; a larger city,
w/ the cooperation

of all sectors

an obvious need
for an all-encompassing plan

lesson of the arrival of the civil service, 1865

what was & still,
a provincial outpost

was then, a lumber town
of working men

considered

to them, "a set of men
who got high salaries

for doing next
to nothing"

of growth, & new
arrival

since

one hundred years,
a number

of derelict mills,
& the vestiges of industry

the rail

barely a communal scar
on all these pristine buildings

address to the federal district commission, 1949

with the greber report, the question becomes,
what does a city make

a capital idea

a man like sparks, or
a man like booth

a greenbelt, reining
progress in

& the creation of a gatineau park,
the castle ruins moved

what wouldnt know for years

his mother too, the mad
prime minister, william lyon

mackenzie king

union station moved, away
from adjoining hotel

the plans once of a canadian pacific,
& the wake of the titanic

instead

a plan for national capital

lesson of the parliament buildings

a city of romantics
& optimists

once

victorian lumber town
building state of the art

& well over budget

centre block plus two in mud,
what landscaping couldnt afford

for some time after

on the most beautiful hill,
they said, in the

western
world

even once the fire,
clock chimes rang

for hours

lecture to lisgar collegiate, graduating class, 1959

to write a praise, to write
a praise of distance

the years i never slept

i know you by your wake, &
absence by

tumble down a concrete steps, in
second year

a second time around

brian nichol, whos first kiss
yours

when fourteen years

on gilmour street, razed
a house & your best friend

to eventual rubble

i want to write a praise,
your trembling hand, you

who was never here
, i want to know

everything i can never
, want to know

just what you missed

lesson of nepean point, 1635

who is & who

hand up to eyes,
a cover

an electric fence

& someone on the hill that you can
barely see

address to the glengarry historical society, 1954

it is not enough to know the world
to own it

not that you could

or know history
to take part in its care

stand
up above the last

suspend
the next fifty years

lesson of the tulip festival

a city of festivals; a city
of something else

where gluehouse pony busked
the front gate; how many

years was that

a decade before starling

a princess born between the war
in secret ottawa, their hospital room

declared dutch soil

& every year a tulip gift,
bulbs & all

                                        out of the longest winter,
when we know the spring,
colour photos

in the *citizen* & *sun*

: a single tulip, breaking through hill snow

acknowledgements:

versions of these pieces (some slightly altered) have appeared previously as various above/ground press broadsides, & in *dig* (ON), *drop* (ON), *GLIMPSE* (ON), *The Centretown Buzz* (ON), *High Altitude Poetry* (BC), *Near South* (IL), *ottawater 3.0* (ON), Walrus (ON), *purdyesque* (Ottawa ON: above/ground press, 2006), & the chapbooks *morning edition* (Ottawa: above/ground press, 2003) & *the address book (erasure)* (above/ground press, 2006), as well as broadcast on CBC Radio's "All in a Day" (Ottawa). "ottawa poems (blue notes)" appeared as an issue of *STANZAS* (above/ground press, 2005); a slightly shorter version was later reprinted by Peter Ganick (West Hartford CT: small chapbook project, 2007). other pieces & fractions have appeared on the author's blog, *www.robmclennan.blogspot.com*

notes:

"the (ottawa) lectures" owes a debt to Stephen Heighton via an interview conducted by Ben Lavigne, via *Matrix* magazine #68 (Montreal QC: fall 2004). "house hold (city) earth" owes a debt to Fred Wah, via an interview conducted by Susan Rudy in *Poets Talk* (Edmonton AB: NeWest Press, 2005). completely random as triggers, but they (inadvertently) sent me spiraling off in interesting directions.

thanks:

for conversations, comments & advice on previous drafts, to Gwendolyn Guth, Stephen Artelle, Jennifer Mulligan, Sandra Ridley, Brendan Hodgson, Rachel Zolf, Roland Prevost, John Lavery, Melanie Little & Peter Norman. Thanks, especially, for Monty Reid for going through the manuscript as a whole, & for continued support, friendship & advice. Thanks to my daughter Kate, who lives this city with me much of the time, whether she is aware of it or not.

Born in Ottawa in 1970 at the Grace Hospital on Wellington Street near Parkdale Avenue, **rob mclennan** currently lives directly between Ottawa's Chinatown and Little Italy neighbourhoods, and was called "Centretown's poet laureate" by David Gladstone in *The Centretown Buzz* in the mid-1990s. The author of twelve previous trade poetry collections in Canada and England, he has published poetry, fiction, interviews, reviews and columns in over two hundred publications in fourteen countries and in four languages, and done reading tours in five countries on two continents. The editor/publisher of above/ground press and the long poem magazine *STANZAS* (both founded in 1993), the online critical journal *Poetics.ca* (with Ottawa poet Stephen Brockwell) and the Ottawa poetry annual *ottawater* (*ottawater.com*), he edits the ongoing Cauldron Books series through Broken Jaw Press, edited the anthologies *evergreen: six new poets* (Black Moss Press), *side/lines: a new canadian poetics* (Insomniac Press), *GROUNDSWELL: the best of above/ground press, 1993-2003* (Broken Jaw Press) and *Decalogue: ten Ottawa poets* (Chaudiere Books), and runs the semi-annual ottawa small press book fair, which he co-founded in 1994, currently under the umbrella of the small press action network - ottawa (span-o), which he also runs. Fall 2007 sees the appearance of a new poetry collection with Ireland's Salmon Publishing, a collection of literary essays appears with Toronto's ECW Press, a novella with The Mercury Press, and a title for Vancouver publisher Arsenal Pulp Press, *Ottawa: The Unknown City*. His online home is at *www.track0.com/rob_mclennan*, and he often posts reviews, essays, rants and other nonsense at *www.robmclennan.blogspot.com*. He was recently named writer-in-residence for the University of Alberta for the 2007-8 academic year.

Other titles from Chaudiere Books

Decalogue: ten Ottawa poets. rob mclennan, editor, 2006. 978-0-9781601-3-5
Disappointment Island. Monty Reid, poetry, 2006. 978-0-9781601-1-1
Movements in Jars. Meghan Jackson, poetry, 2006. 978-0-9781601-0-4
The Desmond Road Book of the Dead. Clare Latremouille, fiction, 2006. 978-0-9781601-2-8